In the Year 1995

By

Kerry Butters.

In the Year 1995

Millennium:	2nd millennium
Centuries:	19th century – **20th century** – 21st century
Decades:	1960s 1970s 1980s – **1990s** – 2000s 2010s 2020s
Years:	1992 1993 1994 – **1995** – 1996 1997 1998

1995 (MCMXCV) was a common year starting on Sunday (dominical letter A) of the Gregorian calendar, the 1995th year of the Common Era (CE) and *Anno Domini* (AD) designations, the 995th year of the 2nd millennium, the 95th year of the 20th century, and the 6th year of the 1990s decade.

This was the year that the Internet entered public consciousness and also the year it was completely privatized and the United States Government no longer funded it with public money - in April **1995** the NSFNET was retired. America Online and Prodigy offered access to the World Wide Web system for the first time this year, releasing browsers that made it easily accessible to the general public.

Contents

Events

January

- January 1
  - The World Trade Organization (WTO) is established to replace the General Agreement on Tariffs and Trade (GATT).
  - Austria, Finland and Sweden act to join the European Union.

- The Draupner wave in the North Sea in Norway is detected, confirming the existence of rogue waves.
- January 6–7 – A chemical fire occurs in an apartment complex in Manila, Philippines. Policemen led by watch commander Aida Fariscal and investigators find a bomb factory and a laptop computer and disks that contain plans for Project Bojinka, a mass-terrorist attack. The mastermind, Ramzi Yousef, is arrested one month later.
- January 9 – Valeri Polyakov completes 366 days in space while aboard the Mir space station, breaking a duration record.
- January 16
  - An avalanche hits the village Súðavík in Iceland, killing 14 people.
  - The fourth *Star Trek* TV series, *Voyager*, premieres on UPN in the United States.
- January 17
  - The 6.9 Mw Great Hanshin earthquake shakes the southern Hyōgo Prefecture with a maximum Shindo of VII, leaving 5,502–6,434 people dead, and 251,301–310,000 displaced.
  - Prodigy (online service) offers access to the World Wide Web.

- January 24 – Opening statements in the O. J. Simpson murder case trial in Los Angeles.
- January 25 – Norwegian rocket incident: A rocket launched from the space exploration centre at Andøya, Norway is briefly interpreted by the Russians as an incoming attack.
- January 30 – John Howard becomes leader of the Liberal Party of Australia to challenge Paul Keating for the 1996 Federal Election and the position of Prime Minister of Australia.
- January 31 – U.S. President Bill Clinton invokes emergency powers, to extend a $20 billion loan to help Mexico avert financial collapse.

February

- February 1 – Lyricist/guitarist Richey Edwards of the Welsh alternative rock band Manic Street Preachers goes missing from a hotel in Bayswater, London on the eve of a planned tour of the United States. His car is found two weeks later at Severn View services in Aust.
- February 9 – *STS-63*: Dr. Bernard A. Harris, Jr. and Michael Foale became the second African American and Briton, respectively, to walk in space.
- February 13 – A United Nations tribunal on human rights violations in the Balkans charges 21 Bosnian

Serb commanders with genocide and crimes against humanity.

- February 15 – Hacker Kevin Mitnick is arrested by the FBI and charged with penetrating some of the United States' most "secure" computer systems.
- February 17
  - Colin Ferguson is convicted of 6 counts of murder for the December 1993 Long Island Rail Road shootings and later receives a 25-year sentence for each of the 6 murders.
- February 21
  - Serkadji prison mutiny in Algeria: Four guards and 96 prisoners are killed in a day and a half.
  - Ibrahim Ali, a 17-year-old Comorian living in France, is murdered by 3 far-right National Front activists.
  - Steve Fossett lands in Leader, Saskatchewan, Canada, becoming the first person to make a solo flight across the Pacific Ocean in a balloon.
- February 23 – The Dow Jones Industrial Average gains 30.28 to close at 4,003.33 – the Dow's first ever close above 4,000.
- February 25 – Amazon Cooperation Treaty Organization (ACTO) (Organización del Tratado de Cooperación Amazónica [OTCA]).

- February 26 – The United Kingdom's oldest investment banking firm, Barings Bank, collapses after securities broker Nick Leeson loses $1.4 billion by speculating on the Tokyo Stock Exchange
- February 27 – In Denver, Colorado, Stapleton Airport closes and is replaced by the new Denver International Airport, the largest in the United States.
- February 28 – Members of the group Patriot's Council are convicted in Minnesota of manufacturing ricin.

March

- March 1
  - Julio María Sanguinetti is sworn in as President of Uruguay for his second term.
  - Polish Prime Minister Waldemar Pawlak resigns from Parliament and is replaced by ex-communist Józef Oleksy.
  - In Moscow, Russian anti-corruption journalist Vladislav Listyev is killed by a gunman.
  - The first Yahoo! Search interface is founded.
- March 2 – Nick Leeson is arrested in Singapore for his role in the collapse of Barings Bank.
- March 3 – In Somalia, the United Nations peacekeeping mission ends.
- March 6 – On an episode of *The Jenny Jones Show* ("Same-Sex Crushes") in the United States, Scott

Amedure reveals a crush on his heterosexual friend Jonathan Schmitz. Schmitz kills Amedure several days after the show.

- March 12 – The Gazi Quarter riots occur in Sultangazi (then Gaziosmanpaşa), Istanbul, Turkey. A few days later, riots break out in Ümraniye, Istanbul and Kızılay, Ankara also.
- March 13 – David Daliberti and William Barloon, Americans working for a military contractor in Kuwait, are arrested after straying into Iraq.
- March 14 – Astronaut Norman Thagard becomes the first American to ride into space aboard a Russian launch vehicle (the *Soyuz TM-21*), lifting off from the Baikonur Cosmodrome in Kazakhstan.
- March 16 – Mississippi ratifies the Thirteenth Amendment, becoming the last state to approve the abolition of slavery. The amendment was nationally ratified in 1865.
- March 20 – Sarin gas attack on the Tokyo subway: Members of the Aum Shinrikyo religious cult release sarin gas on 5 subway trains in Tokyo, killing 13 and injuring 5,510.
- March 22 – Cosmonaut Valeri Polyakov returns after setting a record for 438 days in outer space.
- March 24 – For the first time in 26 years, no British soldiers patrol the streets of Belfast, Northern Ireland.

- March 26 – The Schengen Agreement, easing cross-border travel, goes into effect in several European countries.
- March 30 – A police officer tries to assassinate Takaji Kunimatsu, chief of the National Police Agency of Japan.
- March 31
  - Murder of Selena: Mexican American Tejano pop singer Selena is shot and killed at a Days Inn motel in Corpus Christi, Texas by her former employee, Yolanda Saldívar.
  - TAROM Flight 371 from Bucharest to Brussels crashes shortly after take off killing all 60 people on board.

April

April 1 – Dialog Telekom launches Sri Lanka's first GSM mobile phone network.

- April 2 – An explosion in Gaza kills 8, including a Hamas leader.
- April 5 – The U.S. House of Representatives votes 246–188 to cut taxes for individuals and corporations.
- April 7

- First Chechen War – Samashki massacre: Russian paramilitary troops begin a massacre of at least 250 civilians in Samashki, Chechnya.
- In the United States, House Republicans celebrate passage of most of the Contract with America.
- April 19 – Oklahoma City bombing: 168 people, including 8 Federal Marshals and 19 children, are killed at the Alfred P. Murrah Federal Building and 680 wounded by a bomb set off by Timothy McVeigh and one of his accomplices, Terry Nichols.
- April 24 – A Unabomber bomb kills lobbyist Gilbert Murray in Sacramento, California.
- April 28 – In Daegu, South Korea, a gas explosion at a subway construction site kills 101 people, mostly teenage schoolboys.
- April 30 – The United States government stops funding the NSFNET, making the Internet a wholly privatised system.

May

- May 1
  - Jacques Chirac is elected president of France.
  - Croatian forces launch Operation Flash against rebel Serb forces in western Slavonia.
- May 7 – Finland wins the ice hockey world championship.

- May 10 – At Vaal Reefs gold mine in Orkney, a runaway locomotive falls into a lift shaft onto an ascending cage and causes it to plunge 1,500 feet (460 m) to the bottom of the 6,900 feet (2,100 m) deep shaft, killing 104.
- May 11 – More than 170 countries agree to extend the Nuclear Nonproliferation Treaty indefinitely and without conditions.
- May 13 – An earthquake hits the regions of Kozani and Grevena in Greece, with an intensity of 6.6 on the Richter scale.
- May 14
    - The Dalai Lama proclaims 6-year-old Gedhun Choekyi Nyima as the 11th reincarnation of the Panchen Lama.
    - Team New Zealand wins the America's Cup in San Diego, beating Stars and Stripes 5–0.
- May 16 – Japanese police besiege the headquarters of Aum Shinrikyo near Mount Fuji and arrest cult leader Shoko Asahara.
- May 17 – Shawn Nelson, 35, goes on a tank rampage in San Diego.
- May 20 – U.S. President Bill Clinton indefinitely closes part of the street in front of the White House, Pennsylvania Avenue, to vehicular traffic in response to the Oklahoma City bombing.

- May 21 – Pope John Paul II canonizes John Sarkander during his visit to Olomouc, the Czech Republic.
- May 24 – AFC Ajax wins the UEFA Champions League in the Ernst Happel Stadium in Vienna by defeating AC Milan 0–1 by a goal of Patrick Kluivert. This was the third consecutive win of AFC Ajax over AC Milan that season, ranking AFC Ajax on the 4th place on the list of European Cup and UEFA Champions League winners.
- May 27 – In Culpeper, Virginia, actor Christopher Reeve is paralyzed from the neck down after falling from his horse in a riding competition.
- May 28 – A 7.6 magnitude earthquake in Neftegorsk, Russia kills at least 2,000.

June

- June 1 – The busiest hurricane season in 62 years begins.
- June 2
  - Mrkonjić Grad incident: A United States Air Force F-16 piloted by Captain Scott O'Grady is shot down over Bosnia and Herzegovina while patrolling the NATO no-fly zone. O'Grady is rescued by U.S. Marines six days later.
  - Waffen-SS Hauptsturmführer Erich Priebke is extradited from Argentina to Italy.

- The Dimmitt, Texas Tornado strikes.
- June 3 – Montreal Expos pitcher Pedro Martínez becomes the second Major League Baseball pitcher to pitch a "perfect game" leading into the 10th inning.
- June 6
  - U.S. astronaut Norman Thagard breaks NASA's space endurance record of 14 days, 1 hour and 16 minutes, aboard the Russian space station Mir.
  - The Constitutional Court of South Africa abolishes capital punishment in South Africa in the case of *S v Makwanyane and Another*.
- June 13 – French President Jacques Chirac announces the resumption of nuclear tests in French Polynesia.
- June 15 – A powerful earthquake, registering a moment magnitude of 6.2, hits the city of Aigio, Greece, resulting in several deaths and significant damage to many buildings.
- June 16 – The IOC selects Salt Lake City to host the 2002 Winter Olympics.
- June 20 – Oil multinational Royal Dutch Shell caves in to international pressure and abandons plans to dump the Brent Spar oil rig at sea.
- June 22 – Japanese police rescue 365 hostages from a hijacked All Nippon Airways Flight 857 (Boeing 747-200) at Hakodate airport. The hijacker was armed

with a knife and demanded the release of Shoko Asahara.

- June 24
  - The New Jersey Devils sweep the heavily favored Detroit Red Wings to win their first Stanley Cup in the lock-out shortened season.
  - South Africa wins the Rugby World Cup.
- June 27 – Jodi Huisentruit, an Iowa television anchor, is reported missing after failing to show up for work. She is declared legally dead in 2001.
- June 29
  - Lisa Clayton completes her 10-month solo circumnavigation from the Northern Hemisphere.
  - *STS-71*: Space Shuttle *Atlantis* docks with the Russian Mir space station for the first time.
  - The Sampoong Department Store collapses in the Seocho-gu district of Seoul, South Korea, killing 501 and injuring 937.
  - Iraq disarmament crisis: According to UNSCOM, the unity of the U.N. Security Council begins to fray, as a few countries, particularly France and Russia, become more interested in making financial deals with Iraq than in disarming the country.

July

- July – Iraq disarmament crisis: Iraq threatens to end all cooperation with UNSCOM and IAEA, if sanctions against the country are not lifted by August 31. Following the defection of his son-in-law, Hussein Kamel al-Majid, Saddam Hussein makes new revelations about the full extent of Iraq's biological and nuclear weapons programs. Iraq also withdraws its last U.N. declaration of prohibited biological weapons and turns over a large amount of new documents on its WMD programs.
- July 1 – Iraq disarmament crisis: In response to UNSCOM's evidence, Iraq admits for first time the existence of an offensive biological weapons program, but denies weaponization.
- July 4 – Prime Minister of the United Kingdom John Major wins his battle to remain leader of the Conservative Party.
- July 9 – Sri Lankan Civil War: 125 civilians are killed in Navaly as result of bombing by the Sri Lanka Air Force.
- July 10 – Burmese dissident Aung San Suu Kyi is freed from house arrest.
- July 11

- Srebrenica massacre: Units of the Army of Republika Srpska, under the command of General Ratko Mladić, enter Srebrenica with little resistance from Dutch peacekeepers of the United Nations Protection Force, going on to kill thousands of Bosniak men and boys and rape many women.
- President Clinton announces the restoration of United States–Vietnam relations twenty years after the Vietnam War.
- A Cubana de Aviación Antonov An-24 crashes into the Caribbean off southeast Cuba killing 44 people.

- July 17 – The Nasdaq Composite index closes above the 1,000 mark for the first time.
- July 18 – A series of huge eruptions by the Soufrière Hills volcano sends lava flows and ash falls across a wide area of southern Montserrat.
- July 21–July 26 – Third Taiwan Strait Crisis: The Chinese People's Liberation Army fires missiles into the waters north of Taiwan.
- July 23 – David Daliberti and William Barloon, 2 Americans held as spies by Iraq, are released by Saddam Hussein after negotiations with U.S. Congressman Bill Richardson.

August

- August 2 – The first cold front of the White Earthquake strikes Chile; during the rest of August several communities becomes isolated due to heavy snowfall and livestock is decimated.
- August 3 – An Il-76TD piloted by a Russian crew is forced down by Taliban fighter planes. The crew escape with the aircraft on August 16, 1996.
- August 4 – Croatian forces, with the cooperation of the ARBiH, launch Operation Storm against rebel Croatian Serb forces in the Krajina, which subsequently ceases to exist as a political entity.
- August 5 – Croatian forces take the Croatian Serb capital, Knin, and continue their advance into the Republic of Serbian Krajina.
- August 6 – Hundreds in Hiroshima, Nagasaki, Washington, D.C., and Tokyo mark the 50th anniversary of the dropping of the atomic bomb.
- August 7 – Operation Storm ends with a UN-brokered ceasefire; remaining Croatian Serb forces start surrendering.
- August 11 – The Russell Hill subway accident results in 3 deaths and 30 injuries in Toronto, Ontario, Canada.

- August 14 – An avalanche buries Alison Hargreaves, the first woman to climb Mt. Everest without oxygen; she is reported dead.
- August 16 – Bermudans reject independence in a referendum.
- August 24 – Microsoft releases Windows 95.
- August 28 – A Bosnian Serb mortar bomb near a Sarajevo market square kills 37 civilians.
- August 29 – Eduard Shevardnadze, the Georgian head of state, survives an assassination attempt in Tbilisi.
- August 30 – The NATO bombing campaign against Bosnian Serb artillery positions begins in Bosnia and Herzegovina, continuing into September. At the same time, ARBiH forces begin an offensive against the Bosnian Serb Army around Sarajevo, central Bosnia, and Bosnian Krajina.

September

- September
  - The DVD, an optical disc computer storage media format, is announced.
  - The European Parliament elects the first European Ombudsman, Jacob Söderman, who takes up office in September 1995.
- September 3 – eBay is founded.

- September 4–15 The Fourth World Conference on Women in Beijing with over 4,750 delegates from 181 countries in attendance.
- September 6 – NATO air strikes against Bosnian Serb forces continue, after repeated attempts at a solution to the Bosnian War fail.
- September 19 – *The Washington Post* and *The New York Times* publish the Unabomber's manifesto.
- September 22 – American millionaire Steve Forbes announces his candidacy for the 1996 Republican presidential nomination.
- September 23 – Argentine national Guillermo "Bill" Gaede is arrested in Phoenix, Arizona on charges of industrial espionage. His sales to Cuba, China, North Korea and Iran are believed to have involved Intel and AMD trade secrets worth US$10–20 million.
- September 26 – The trial against former Italian Prime Minister Giulio Andreotti, who is accused of Mafia connections, begins.
- September 27–September 28 – Bob Denard's mercenaries capture President Said Mohammed Djohor of the Comoros; the local army does not resist.
- September 28 – Croatian forces massacre 9 elderly Croatian Serbs in the village of Varivode, Croatia

October

- October 3 – O. J. Simpson is found not guilty of double murder for the deaths of former wife Nicole Simpson and Ronald Goldman.
- October 4
  - France launches a counter-coup in the Comoros with 600 soldiers. They arrest Bob Denard and his mercenaries and take Denard to France; Caabi el-Yachroutu becomes the interim president.
  - Hurricane Opal makes landfall at Pensacola Beach, Florida as a Category 3 hurricane with 115 mph (185 km/h) winds.
- October 5 – Tansu Çiller of DYP forms the new government of Turkey (51st government, a minority government which failed to receive the vote of confidence).
- October 6 – Michel Mayor and Didier Queloz announce the discovery of 51 Pegasi b, the first confirmed extrasolar planet orbiting an ordinary main-sequence star.
- October 9 – 1995 Palo Verde derailment: An Amtrak Sunset Limited train is derailed by saboteurs near Palo Verde, Arizona.

- October 15 – The Carolina Panthers win their first-ever regular season game by defeating the New York Jets at Clemson Memorial Stadium in South Carolina.
- October 16 – The Million Man March is held in Washington, D.C. The event was conceived by Nation of Islam leader Louis Farrakhan.
- October 17 – French woman Jeanne Calment reaches the confirmed age of 120 years and 238 days, making her the oldest person ever recorded.
- October 23 – In Houston, Texas, Yolanda Saldívar is convicted of first degree murder in the shooting death of Selena Quintanilla Perez, and 3 days later is sentenced to life in prison.
- October 24 – A total solar eclipse is visible from Iran, India, Thailand, and Southeast Asia.
- October 25 – A Metra commuter train slams into a school bus in Fox River Grove, Illinois, killing seven students.
- October 26 – An avalanche hits the village Flateyri in Iceland, killing 20 people.
- October 28 – A fire in Baku Metro, Azerbaijan, kills 289 passengers (the world's worst subway disaster).
- October 30
  - Quebec independentists narrowly lose a referendum for a mandate to negotiate independence from Canada.

- o Tansu Çiller of DYP forms the new government of Turkey.

November

- November 1
  - o NASA loses contact with the Pioneer 11 probe.
  - o Participants in the Yugoslav Wars begin negotiations at the Wright-Patterson Air Force Base in Dayton, Ohio.
  - o The U.S. House of Representatives votes to ban partial birth abortions by a vote of 288–139.
- November 2 – The Supreme Court of Argentina orders the extradition of Erich Priebke, ex-S.S. captain.
- November 3 – At Arlington National Cemetery, U.S. President Bill Clinton dedicates a memorial to the victims of the Pan Am Flight 103 bombing.
- November 4 – Israeli Prime Minister Yitzhak Rabin is assassinated at a peace rally in Tel Aviv.
- November 7 – Typhoon Angela leaves the Philippines and Vietnam devastated, with 882 deaths and damage of P 10,829,000,000. The typhoon was the strongest ever to strike the Philippines in 25 years, with wind speeds of 130 mph (210 km/h) and gusts of 180 mph (290 km/h).
- November 10

- Iraq disarmament crisis: With help from Israel and Jordan, UNSCOM inspector Scott Ritter intercepts 240 Russian gyroscopes and accelerometers on their way to Iraq from Russia.
- In Nigeria, playwright and environmental activist Ken Saro-Wiwa, along with 8 others from the Movement for the Survival of the Ogoni People, are hanged by government forces.

- November 12 – The Millbrook Commonwealth Action Programme, a programme to implement the Harare Declaration, is announced by the Commonwealth Heads of Government.
- November 14 – A budget standoff between Democrats and Republicans in the Congress of the United States, forces the federal government to temporarily close national parks and museums, and run most government offices with skeleton staff.
- November 16 – A United Nations tribunal charges Radovan Karadžić and Ratko Mladić with genocide during the Bosnian War.
- November 21
  - The Dow Jones Industrial Average gains 40.46 to close at 5,023.55, its first close above 5,000. This makes 1995 the first year where the Dow surpasses two millennium marks in a single year.

- The Dayton Agreement to end the Bosnian War is reached at Wright-Patterson Air Force Base near Dayton, Ohio (signed December 14).
- November 22
  - Rosemary West is sentenced to life for killing 10 women and girls, including her daughter and stepdaughter, after the jury returns a guilty verdict at Winchester Crown Court. The trial judge recommends that she should never be released from prison, making her only the second woman in British legal history to be subjected to a whole life tariff (the other is Myra Hindley).
  - Six-year-old Elisa Izquierdo's child abuse-related death at the hands of her mother makes headlines, and instigates major reform in New York City's child welfare system.
  - Egypt, Eilat, Israel, and much of the North African Mediterranean is struck by the strongest earthquake (7.2 M_w) along the Dead Sea Transform in a century; 8 are killed.
  - The first-ever full length computer animated feature film, *Toy Story*, is released by Pixar Animation Studios and Walt Disney Pictures.
- November 28
  - The Barcelona Treaty is signed by 27 attending nations.

- U.S. President Bill Clinton signs the National Highway System Designation Act of 1995, which ends the federal 55 mph (89 km/h) speed limit.
- November 30 – Javier Solana becomes the new NATO General Secretary; Operation Desert Storm officially ends.

December

- December 3 – Strikes paralyze France's public sector.
- December 7 – NASA's *Galileo Probe* enters Jupiter's atmosphere.
- December 8
  - Jean-Dominique Bauby, editor-in-chief of *Elle* magazine, suffers a massive stroke and lapses into a coma.
  - 6-year-old Gyaincain Norbu is enthroned as the 11th reincarnation of the Panchen Lama at Tashilhunpo Monastery.
- December 14 – The Dayton Agreement is signed in Paris.
- December 15
  - The European Court of Justice rules that all EU football players have the right to a free transfer among member states at the end of their contracts.

- Because of the "quadruple-witching" option expiration, volume on the New York Stock Exchange hits 638 million shares, the highest single-day volume since October 20, 1987, when the Dow staged a stunning recovery a day after Black Monday.
- December 16 – Iraq disarmament crisis: Iraqi scuba divers, under the direction of the United Nations Special Commission, dredge the Tigris near Baghdad. The divers find over 200 prohibited Russian-made missile instruments and components.
- December 20
  - American Airlines Flight 965 (Boeing 757) crashes into a mountain near Buga, Valle del Cauca, Colombia after veering off its course en route to Cali, Colombia. Of the 164 people on board, 4 passengers are the only survivors.
  - HM The Queen advises "an early divorce" to Lady Diana Spencer and Charles, Prince of Wales. The divorce is finalized on 28 August 1996.
- December 30
  - The lowest ever United Kingdom temperature of −27.2 °C (−17.0 °F) is recorded at Altnaharra in the Scottish Highlands. This equals the record set at Braemar, Aberdeenshire in 1895 and 1982.

- The Republic of Texas group claims to have formed a provisional government in Texas.
- December 31 – The final original *Calvin and Hobbes* comic strip is published.

Date unknown

- Sudden oak death, the tree disease caused by the plant pathogen *Phytophthora ramorum*, is first observed, in California.

Births

January

- January 1 – Sardar Azmoun, Iranian footballer
- January 3
  - Muhammed Demirci, Turkish footballer
  - Victoria Duffield, Canadian pop singer
  - Kim Seolhyun, member of South Korean group AOA
- January 4
  - Maddie Hasson, American actress
  - María Isabel, Spanish singer

- January 9 – Nicola Peltz, American actress
- January 17 – Ann Li, Taiwanese actress
- January 20
  - Joey Badass, American rapper
  - Calum Chambers, English footballer
- January 21 – Jennifer Rae Daykin, British teen actress
- January 24
  - Callan McAuliffe, Australian actor
  - Dylan Everett, Canadian actor
- January 26 – Kyle Chavarria, American actress
- January 30
  - Danielle Campbell, American actress
  - Viktoria Komova, Russian artistic gymnast
  - Thia Megia, American singer
- January 31 – Nina Sublatti, Georgian singer, songwriter, calligrapher and model

February

- February 5
  - Rouguy Diallo, French triple jumper
  - Adnan Januzaj, Belgian footballer
- February 6
  - Moon Jong-up, South Korean singer and dancer
  - Nyck de Vries, Dutch kart racer
- February 8 – Jordan Todosey, Canadian actress

- February 13
  - Marsel Efroimski, Israeli chess player
  - Ayame Koike, Japanese actress
- February 14 – Diego Fagúndez, American footballer
- February 23 – Andrew Wiggins, Canadian basketball player
- February 26 – Liam Fairhurst, British charity fundraiser (d.2009)
- February 28 – Madisen Beaty, American actress

March

- March 2 – Mats Møller Dæhli, Norwegian footballer
- March 3 – Maine Mendoza, Filipino actress, internet celebrity, comedianne, and television host (AlDub)
- March 7 – Hailey Clauson, American model
- March 8 – Luca Brecel, Belgian snooker player
- March 12 – Kanon Fukuda, Japanese pop singer and voice actress
- March 13 – Mikaela Shiffrin, American skier, World Champion Slalom 2013
- March 15 – Jabari Parker, American basketball player
- March 16 – Shy Carlos, Filipino actress
- March 19
  - Philip Daniel Bolden, American actor
  - Héctor Bellerín, Spanish footballer

- March 21 – Diggy Simmons, American rapper
- March 22 – Nick Robinson, American actor
- March 27 – Taylor Atelian, American actress

April

- April 14 – Yukiko Fujisawa, Japanese figure skater
- April 15 – Kiri Baga, American figure skater
- April 17 – Kirk Knight, American rapper and record producer
- April 18 – Divock Origi, Belgian footballer
- April 23 – Gigi Hadid, American model
- April 24
  - Axel Chapelle, French pole vaulter
  - Kehlani, American singer-songwriter
- April 26 – Daniel Padilla, Filipino actor
- April 28 – Yulia Gurska, Ukrainian singer-songwriter

May

- May 2 – Skye Bennett, English actress
- May 3 – Celeste Buckingham, Slovak singer-songwriter

- May 4 – Martin Santiago Augusto Castillo, Argentine boxer
- May 5 – Devon Gearhart, American actor
- May 10 – Missy Franklin, American swimmer
- May 12
  - Luke Benward, American actor and singer
  - Kenton Duty, American actor
- May 14 – Kelly Gale, Swedish model
- May 15 – Ksenia Sitnik, Belarusian singer
- May 25 – Greg Grossman, American chef
- May 28 – Jacob Kogan, American actor

June

- June 2 – Sterling Beaumon, American actor
- June 4 – Jerome Ponce, Filipino actor
- June 5
  - Beckii Cruel, British pop dancer
  - Trentavis Friday, American sprinter
  - Troye Sivan, Australian actor
- June 8
  - Bessie Cursons, English actress
  - Akari Saho, Japanese musician
- June 9 – Alina Grosu, Ukrainian singer
- June 22 – Wilhem Belocian, French sprinter
- June 23 – Eva Lazzaro, Australian actress
- June 27 – Eirik Gjen, Norwegian artist

- June 28 – Kåre Hedebrant, Swedish actor

July

- July 7 – Chloe Greenfield, American actress
- July 9 – Georgie Henley, English actress
- July 10
  - Trayvon Bromell, American sprinter
  - Edymar Martínez, Venezuelan model and Miss International 2015 titleholder
- July 12 – Jordyn Wieber, American gymnast
- July 14 – Serge Gnabry, German footballer
- July 15 – Elyar Fox, British singer
- July 19
  - María José Alvarado, Honduran model (d. 2014)
  - Maria Paseka, Russian artistic gymnast
- July 26 – Holly Bodimeade, British actress

August

- August 1 – Derrick Monasterio, Filipino actor, dancer and singer
- August 4
  - Bruna Marquezine, Brazilian actress
  - Jessica Sanchez, American singer
- August 15 – Chief Keef, American rapper

- August 20 – Liana Liberato, American actress
- August 23 – Tommy Batchelor, American dancer

September

- September 1 – Nathan MacKinnon, Canadian hockey player
- September 5
  - Tehilla Blad, Swedish actress
  - Caroline Sunshine, American actress
- September 6 – Bertrand Traoré, Burkinabé footballer
- September 8 – Thuliso Dingwall, American actor
- September 12 – Ryan Potter, American actor
- September 13 – Robbie Kay, British actor
- September 20
  - Laura Dekker, Dutch solo sailor
  - Sammi Hanratty, American actress
- September 22 – Juliette Goglia, American actress

October

- October 8 – Courtney Taylor Burness, American actress
- October 12 – Claudio Encarnacion Montero, English actor
- October 15 – Billy Unger, American actor and martial artist

- October 20 – Wang Zhenwei, Chinese actor and martial artist
- October 21 – Antoinette Guedia Mouafo, Cameroonian swimmer
- October 23 – Ireland Baldwin, American model
- October 25 – Conchita Campbell, Canadian actress

November

- November 1
  - Nick D'Aloisio, British computer programmer
  - Nour El Sherbini, Egyptian squash player
- November 3 – Kendall Jenner, American model and reality television personality
- November 7 – Michael Dameski, Australian dancer and actor
- November 16 – Noah Gray-Cabey, American actor and pianist
- November 16 – Changjo, South Korean dancer, singer and actor
- November 29 – Laura Marano, American actress and singer

December

- December 4 – Dina Asher-Smith, British sprinter
- December 6 – Joy Gruttmann, German singer
- December 8 – Jordon Ibe, English footballer
- December 9 – McKayla Maroney, American gymnast
- December 14 – Yulia Belokobylskaya, Russian gymnast
- December 15 – Yoshihide Kiryū, Japanese sprinter
- December 19 – Elliot Evans, English singer
- December 20 – Feliks Zemdegs, Australian Rubik's Cube speedsolver
- December 22 – Hunter Allan, American actor
- December 26 – Zach Mills, American actor
- December 29 – Ross Lynch, American actor
- December 31 – Gabby Douglas, American gymnast

Deaths

January

- January 1
  - Fred West, English serial killer (b. 1941)
  - Eugene Wigner, Hungarian physicist, Nobel Prize laureate (b. 1902)
- January 2
  - Siad Barre, Military dictator of Somalia (b. 1919)
  - Nancy Kelly, American actress (b. 1921)
  - Ephraim Amu, Ghanaian composer, musicologist and teacher (b. 1899)
- January 4 – Sol Tax, American anthropologist (b. 1907)
- January 7
  - Murray Rothbard, American economist (b. 1926)
  - Larry Grayson, British comedian and game show host (b. 1923)
- January 9 – Peter Cook, English comedian and writer (b. 1937)
- January 11, Onat Kutlar, Turkish writer, poet, screenplay writer, founder of Turkish Sinematek (b. 1936)
- January 15, Frederick J. Schlink, American consumer rights activist (b. 1891)

- January 18
  - Adolf Butenandt, German chemist, Nobel Prize laureate (b. 1903)
  - Ron Luciano, American baseball umpire (b. 1937)
- January 22
  - Jerry Blackwell, American professional wrestler (b. 1949)
  - Rose Fitzgerald Kennedy, American philanthropist and mother of President John F. Kennedy (b. 1890)
- January 24 – David Cole, American record producer and songwriter, half of the duo C+C Music Factory (b. 1962)
- January 26 – Geoffrey Parsons, Australian pianist (b. 1929)
- January 29 – Song Sung-il, South Korean wrestler (b. 1969)
- January 30 – Gerald Durrell, British naturalist, zookeeper, author, and television presenter (b. 1925)
- January 31 – George Abbott, American writer, director, and producer (b. 1887)

February

- February 2
  - Fred Perry, English tennis champion (b. 1909)
  - Donald Pleasence, English actor (b. 1919)

- February 4 – Patricia Highsmith, American author (b. 1921)
- February 5 – Doug McClure, American actor (b. 1935)
- February 6 – James Merrill, American poet (b. 1926)
- February 8 – Rachel Thomas, Welsh actress (b. 1905)
- February 9 – David Wayne, American actor (b. 1914)
- February 12
  - Robert Bolt, English writer (b. 1924)
  - Jacob Rader Marcus, scholar of Jewish history and a Reform rabbi (b. 1896)
  - Philip Taylor Kramer, American musician (b. 1952)
- February 14 – U Nu, Burmese politician (b. 1907)
- February 19
  - Sir Nicholas Fairbairn, British politician (b. 1933)
  - John Howard, American actor (b. 1913)
  - Nigel Findley, American role-playing game designer (b. 1959)
- February 22 – Ed Flanders, American actor (b. 1934)
- February 23
  - Melvin Franklin, American singer (b. 1942)
  - James Herriot, English veterinarian and author (b. 1916)
- February 24
  - Tatsumi Kumashiro, Japanese film director (b. 1927)

- Hideko Maehata, Japanese swimmer (b. 1914)
- February 26 – Jack Clayton, British film director (b. 1921)

March

- March 1 – Vladislav Listyev, Russian journalist (b. 1956).
- March 2 – Sasha Krasny, Russian poet and songwriter (b. 1882)
- March 3 – Howard W. Hunter, American Mormon leader (b. 1907)
- March 5 – Vivian Stanshall, English comedian, writer, artist, broadcaster, and musician (b. 1943)
- March 7 – Georges J. F. Köhler, German biologist, recipient of the Nobel Prize in Physiology or Medicine (b. 1946)
- March 8 – Ingo Schwichtenberg, German drummer (b. 1965)
- March 9 – Edward Bernays, Austrian-American pioneer in the field of public relations and propaganda (b. 1891)
- March 11
  - Alf Goullet, Australian cyclist who won more than 400 races on three continents (b. 1891)
  - Isabel Letham, Australian pioneer surfboard rider and swimming instructor (b. 1899)

- March 12 – Juanin Clay, American actress (b. 1949)
- March 13
    - Leon Day, American baseball player (b. 1916)
    - Odette Hallowes, French World War II heroine (b. 1912)
- March 14 – William Alfred Fowler, American physicist, Nobel Prize laureate (b. 1911)
- March 16 – Albert Hackett, American dramatist and screenwriter (b. 1900)
- March 17
    - Rick Aviles, American actor (b. 1952)
    - Ronald Kray, British organised crime leader (b. 1933)
- March 18 – Robin Jacques, English illustrator (b. 1920)
- March 19
    - Nike Ardilla, Indonesian singer (b. 1975)
    - Yasuo Yamada, Japanese voice actor (b. 1932)
- March 20
    - Sidney Kingsley, American dramatist (b. 1906)
    - John William Minton American Wrestler (Big John Studd) (b. 1948)
- March 22 – Peter Woods, British journalist, reporter and newsreader (b. 1930)
- March 23 – Davie Cooper, Scottish footballer (b. 1956)
- March 26 – Eazy-E, American rapper and record producer (b. 1963)

- March 27 – Maurizio Gucci, Italian businessman (b. 1948)
- March 28
    - Hugh O'Connor, American actor the son of Carroll O'Connor (b. 1962)
    - Hanns-Joachim Friedrichs, German journalist (b. 1927)
- March 29
    - Charles Fern, barnstorming Hawaii aviator and newspaper pioneer (b. 1892)
    - Tony Lock, English cricketer (b. 1929)
    - Jimmy McShane (aka Baltimora), Northern Irish dancer (b. 1957)
- March 31 – Selena, Mexican American singer (b. 1971)

April

- April 2
    - Hannes Alfvén, Swedish chemist, Nobel-prize (b.1908)
    - Harvey Penick, American golfer (b. 1904)
- April 3 – Lang Jingshan, Chinese master photographer (b. 1892)
- April 4
    - Kenny Everett, British comedian (b. 1944)

- Priscilla Lane, American actress (b. 1915)
  - Wang Baosen, vice mayor of Beijing, suicide (b. 1935)
- April 10
  - Morarji Desai, Indian politician (b. 1896)
  - Glyn Jones, Welsh writer (b. 1905)
- April 14 – Burl Ives, American singer and actor (b. 1909)
- April 15
  - Jock Robson, Scottish football goalkeeper (b. 1899)
  - Harry Shoulberg, American painter and serigrapher (b. 1903)
- April 16 – Cy Endfield, American screenwriter (b. 1914)
- April 18 – Arturo Frondizi, President of Argentina (b. 1908)
- April 20 – Milovan Đilas, Yugoslavian Marxist (b. 1911)
- April 23 – Howard Cosell, American sportscaster (b. 1918)
- April 24
  - Lodewijk Bruckman, Dutch painter (b. 1903)
  - Art Fleming, American actor and game show host (b. 1924)
- April 25

- Andrea Fortunato, Italian football player (b. 1971)
- Alexander Knox, Canadian actor (b. 1907)
- Ginger Rogers, American actress and dancer (b. 1911)
- Lev Shankovsky, Ukrainian military historian (b. 1903)

May

- May 1 – Antonio Salemme, Italian-born American artist (b. 1895)
- May 2
  - Michael Hordern, English actor (b. 1911)
  - Werner Veigel, German journalist and news presenter (b. 1928)
- May 5
  - Ye Qianyu, Chinese painter and manhua artist (b. 1907)
  - Mikhail Botvinnik, Russian chess player (b. 1911)
  - Al Sanders, American news anchorman (b. 1941)
- May 6 – Noel Brotherston, Irish footballer (b. 1956)
- May 8 – Teresa Teng, Taiwanese singer (b. 1953)
- May 9 – Marguerite Jones, Canadian professional baseball player (b. 1917)
- May 12
  - Arnold Goodman, Baron Goodman, British lawyer and political adviser (b. 1915)

- ○ Arthur Lubin, American film director (b. 1898)
- May 14 – Christian B. Anfinsen, American chemist, Nobel Prize laureate (b. 1916)
- May 15
  - ○ Ben Bubar, American activist (b. 1917)
  - ○ Eric Porter, English actor (b. 1928)
  - ○ Woldeab Woldemariam, Eritrean Politician (b. 1905)
- May 18
  - ○ Elisha Cook, Jr., American actor (b. 1903)
  - ○ Alexander Godunov, Russian-born ballet dancer and actor (b. 1949)
  - ○ Elizabeth Montgomery, American actress (b. 1933)
- May 24
  - ○ Dan Fortmann, American football player (Chicago Bears) and member of the Pro Football Hall of Fame (b. 1916)
  - ○ Harold Wilson, Prime Minister of the United Kingdom (b. 1916)
- May 25 – Jack Allen, English actor (b. 1907)
- May 26 – Friz Freleng, American animator (b. 1906)
- May 27 – Severn Darden, American actor (b. 1929)
- May 28 – Irfan Ljubijankić, Bosnian diplomat (b. 1952)
- May 29 – Margaret Chase Smith, American politician (b. 1897)

- May 30 – Ted Drake, English footballer (b. 1912)

June

- June 3
  - Adolph Lowe, German sociologist and economist (b. 1893)
  - Frank Waters, American Writer (b. 1902)
- June 7 – Hsuan Hua, Chinese Buddhist master (b. 1918)
- June 12 – Arturo Benedetti Michelangeli, Italian pianist (b. 1920)
- June 14
  - Rory Gallagher, Irish blues-guitarist, singer-songwriter and Taste frontman (b. 1948)
  - Roger Zelazny, American writer of fantasy (b. 1937)
  - Saidye Rosner Bronfman, matriarch of the Canadian-Jewish Bronfman family (b. 1897)
- June 15 – Charles Bennett, English screenwriter (b. 1899)
- June 20 – Emil Cioran, Romanian philosopher and essayist (b. 1911)
- June 23 – Jonas Salk, American medical researcher (b. 1914)
- June 25

- ○ Warren E. Burger, Chief Justice of the United States (b. 1907)
  - ○ Ernest Walton, Irish physicist, Nobel Prize laureate (b. 1903)
- June 29 – Lana Turner, American actress (b. 1921)
- June 30
  - ○ Georgi Beregovoi, Russian cosmonaut (b. 1921)
  - ○ Gale Gordon, American actor (b. 1906)

July

- July 1 – Wolfman Jack, American disc jockey (b. 1938)
- July 2 – George Seldes, American investigative journalist and media critic (b. 1890)
- July 3 – Pancho Gonzales, American tennis champion (b. 1928)
- July 4
  - ○ Eva Gabor, Hungarian actress (b. 1919)
  - ○ Bob Ross, American television painter (b. 1942)
- July 5 – Takeo Fukuda, Japanese politician (b. 1905)
- July 16
  - ○ Patsy Ruth Miller, American actress (b. 1904)
  - ○ Stephen Spender, English poet and writer (b. 1909)
- July 17
  - ○ Juan Manuel Fangio, Argentine race car driver (b. 1911)

- Harry Guardino, American actor (b. 1925)
- July 18 – Fabio Casartelli, Italian cyclist (b. 1970)
- July 19 – Tomas Mendez, Mexican composer (b. 1921)
- July 20 – Genevieve Tobin, American actress (b. 1899)
- July 22 – Otakar Borůvka, Czech mathematician best known today for his work in graph theory (b. 1899)
- July 24
  - Marjorie Cameron, American writer, painter, actress, and occultist (b. 1922)
  - George Rodger, British photojournalist (b. 1908)
- July 25 – Charlie Rich, American singer (b. 1932)
- July 27
  - Rick Ferrell, American baseball player (Washington Senators, St. Louis Browns) and member of the MLB Hall of Fame (b. 1905)
  - Miklós Rózsa, Hungarian composer (b. 1907)
- July 29 – Philippe De Lacy, American actor (b. 1917)

August

- August 1 – Esther Muir, American actress (b. 1903)
- August 3
  - Ida Lupino, English-American actress (b. 1918)
  - Edward Whittemore, American author and Central Intelligence agent (b. 1933)
- August 4 – J. Howard Marshall, American billionaire (b. 1905)

- August 7 – Brigid Brophy, English author (b. 1929)
- August 9 – Jerry Garcia, American guitarist (b. 1942)
- August 11
  - Phil Harris, American actor (b. 1904)
  - Herbert Sumsion, English musician (b. 1899)
- August 12 – Felipe Tromp, 1st Governor of Aruba (b. 1917)
- August 13 – Mickey Mantle, American baseball player (New York Yankees) and member of the MLB Hall of Fame (b. 1931)
- August 15 – John Cameron Swayze, American journalist (b. 1906)
- August 17 – Howard Koch, American screenwriter (b. 1901)
- August 19 – Pierre Schaeffer, French composer (b. 1910)
- August 21 – Subrahmanyan Chandrasekhar, Indian-born astrophysicist, Nobel Prize laureate (b. 1910)
- August 22 – Johnny Carey, Irish football player and manager (b. 1919)
- August 24
  - Gary Crosby, American singer and actor (b. 1933)
  - Alfred Eisenstaedt, German-American photographer (b. 1898)
- August 29
  - Michael Ende, German author (b. 1929)

- Frank Perry, American film director (b. 1930)
- August 30
  - Fischer Black, American economist (b. 1938)
  - Sterling Morrison, American guitarist (b. 1942)

September

- September 5 – Benyamin Sueb, Indonesian actor, comedian and singer (b. 1939)
- September 7 – Russell Johnson, cartoonist (b. 1893)
- September 12
  - Jeremy Brett, English actor (b. 1933)
  - Lubomír Beneš, Czech animator and director (b. 1935)
- September 15
  - Harry Calder, South African cricketer (b. 1901)
  - Dietrich Hrabak, German World War II flying ace (b. 1914)
  - Gunnar Nordahl, Swedish footballer (b. 1921)
- September 17 – Grady Sutton, American actor (b. 1906)
- September 19 – Orville Redenbacher, American entrepreneur and businessman (b. 1907)
- September 20 – Eileen Chang, Chinese writer (b. 1920)
- September 25
  - Annie Elizabeth Delany, American dentist and civil rights (b. 1891)

- Dorothy Dickson, American actress and singer (b. 1893)
- Kei Tomiyama, Japanese actor, voice actor, and narrator (b. 1938)
- September 29 – Madalyn Murray O'Hair, American atheist activist (b. 1919)
  - Pedro Nolasco, Dominican boxer (b. 1963)

October

- October 1 – Margaret Gorman, First Miss America winner (b. 1905)
- October 5 – Linda Gary, American voice actress (b. 1944)
- October 9 – Alec Douglas-Home, Prime Minister of the United Kingdom (b. 1903)
- October 21
  - Maxene Andrews, American singer (b. 1916)
  - Jesús Blasco, Spanish comic book author (b. 1919)
  - Shannon Hoon, American singer (Blind Melon) (b. 1967)
- October 22
  - Kingsley Amis, English writer (b. 1922)
  - Mary Wickes, American actress (b. 1910)
  - Li Shouheng, Chinese educator (b. 1898)
- October 25
  - Viveca Lindfors, Swedish actress (b. 1920)

- Bobby Riggs, American tennis champion and promoter (b. 1918)
- October 26
  - Gorni Kramer, Italian bandleader and songwriter (b. 1913)
  - Wilhelm Freddie, Danish painter (b. 1909)
- October 29 – Terry Southern, American screenwriter (b. 1924)

November

- November 1 – W. E. D. Ross, Canadian writer (b. 1912)
- November 4
  - Yitzhak Rabin, Prime Minister of Israel, recipient of the Nobel Peace Prize (b. 1922)
  - Gilles Deleuze, French philosopher (b. 1925)
  - Paul Eddington, English actor (b. 1927)
- November 6 – Aneta Corsaut, American actress (b. 1933)
- November 7 – Ann Dunham, American anthropologist and mother of Barack Obama, the 44th President of the United States (b. 1942)
- November 12 – Robert Stephens, British actor (b. 1931)
- November 13 – Ralph Blane, American composer (b. 1914)

- November 20 – Sergei Grinkov, Russian figure skater (b. 1967)
- November 21
  - Bruno Gerussi, Canadian actor who played Nick Adonidas on TV's "The Beachcombers" (b. 1928)
  - Noel Jones, British diplomat (b. 1940)
- November 22 – Elisa Izquierdo, American murder victim (b. 1989)
- November 23 – Louis Malle, French film director (b. 1932)
- November 24 – Jeffrey Lynn, American actor (b. 1909)
- November 26 – Wim Thoelke, German TV entertainer (b. 1927)
- November 30 – Stretch, American rapper and record producer (b. 1968)

December

- December 2
  - Roxie Roker, American actress (b. 1929)
  - Robertson Davies, Canadian novelist (b. 1913)
- December 3 – Jimmy Jewel, English actor (b. 1909)
- December 7 – Kathleen Harrison, British actress (b. 1892)
- December 9 – Vivian Blaine, American actress (b. 1921)

- December 10 – Darren Robinson, American rapper and actor (b. 1967)
- December 11 – Abolhassan Sadighi, Iranian sculptors and painters (b. 1894)
- December 16 – Johnny Moss, American poker player (b. 1907)
- December 18 – Konrad Zuse, German engineer (b. 1910)
- December 20 – Madge Sinclair, Jamaican-American actress (b. 1938)
- December 22
    - Butterfly McQueen, American actress (b. 1911)
    - James Meade, English economist, Nobel Prize laureate (b. 1907)
- December 23 – Patric Knowles, English actor (b. 1911)
- December 25
    - Nicolas Slonimsky, Russian-American musicologist (b. 1894)
    - Dean Martin, American actor, singer, comedian, and entertainer (b. 1917)
- December 28 – Virginius Dabney, American teacher, writer, journalist and editor (b. 1901)
- December 30
    - Doris Grau, American actress (b. 1924)
    - Heiner Müller, German poet and playwright (b. 1929)

- December 31 – Eduardo Hernández Moncada, Mexican composer, pianist, and conductor (b. 1899)

Nobel Prizes

- Physics – Martin L. Perl, Frederick Reines
- Chemistry – Paul J. Crutzen, Mario J. Molina, F. Sherwood Rowland
- Medicine – Edward B. Lewis, Christiane Nüsslein-Volhard, Eric F. Wieschaus
- Literature – Seamus Heaney
- Bank of Sweden Prize in Economic Sciences in Memory of Alfred Nobel – Robert Lucas, Jr.
- Peace – Joseph Rotblat and the Pugwash Conferences on Science and World Affairs

In the News.

Syria has Peace talks with Israel.

US Imposes economic sanctions against Iran.

A magnitude 7.3 earthquake occurs near Kobe, Japan, killing 6,433 people.

Terrorists release Sarin nerve Gas at Kasumigaseki station killing 12 and sending over 5,000 to hospital.

OJ Simpson is found innocent.

Ebay started the online auction and shopping website.

Popular Films - Toy Story, Batman Forever, Apollo 13, Pocahontas, Ace Ventura: When Nature Calls, GoldenEye.

1995 Calendar.

January 1995
Sun	Mon	Tue	Wed	Thu	Fri	Sat
1	2	3	4	5	6	7
8	9	10	11	12	13	14
15	16	17	18	19	20	21
22	23	24	25	26	27	28
29	30	31				

February 1995
Sun	Mon	Tue	Wed	Thu	Fri	Sat
			1	2	3	4
5	6	7	8	9	10	11
12	13	14	15	16	17	18
19	20	21	22	23	24	25
26	27	28				

March 1995
Sun	Mon	Tue	Wed	Thu	Fri	Sat
			1	2	3	4
5	6	7	8	9	10	11
12	13	14	15	16	17	18
19	20	21	22	23	24	25
26	27	28	29	30	31	

April 1995
Sun	Mon	Tue	Wed	Thu	Fri	Sat
						1
2	3	4	5	6	7	8
9	10	11	12	13	14	15
16	17	18	19	20	21	22
23	24	25	26	27	28	29
30						

May 1995
Sun	Mon	Tue	Wed	Thu	Fri	Sat
	1	2	3	4	5	6
7	8	9	10	11	12	13
14	15	16	17	18	19	20
21	22	23	24	25	26	27
28	29	30	31			

June 1995
Sun	Mon	Tue	Wed	Thu	Fri	Sat
				1	2	3
4	5	6	7	8	9	10
11	12	13	14	15	16	17
18	19	20	21	22	23	24
25	26	27	28	29	30	

July 1995
Sun	Mon	Tue	Wed	Thu	Fri	Sat
						1
2	3	4	5	6	7	8
9	10	11	12	13	14	15
16	17	18	19	20	21	22
23	24	25	26	27	28	29
30	31					

August 1995
Sun	Mon	Tue	Wed	Thu	Fri	Sat
		1	2	3	4	5
6	7	8	9	10	11	12
13	14	15	16	17	18	19
20	21	22	23	24	25	26
27	28	29	30	31		

September 1995
Sun	Mon	Tue	Wed	Thu	Fri	Sat
					1	2
3	4	5	6	7	8	9
10	11	12	13	14	15	16
17	18	19	20	21	22	23
24	25	26	27	28	29	30

October 1995
Sun	Mon	Tue	Wed	Thu	Fri	Sat
1	2	3	4	5	6	7
8	9	10	11	12	13	14
15	16	17	18	19	20	21
22	23	24	25	26	27	28
29	30	31				

November 1995
Sun	Mon	Tue	Wed	Thu	Fri	Sat
			1	2	3	4
5	6	7	8	9	10	11
12	13	14	15	16	17	18
19	20	21	22	23	24	25
26	27	28	29	30		

December 1995
Sun	Mon	Tue	Wed	Thu	Fri	Sat
					1	2
3	4	5	6	7	8	9
10	11	12	13	14	15	16
17	18	19	20	21	22	23
24	25	26	27	28	29	30
31